My Thoughts and Experiences as a Pet Sitter

by
Ruth M. Petrucci

Cork Hill Press
Carmel

Cork Hill Press
597 Industrial Drive, Suite 110
Carmel, IN 46032-4207
1-866-688-BOOK
www.corkhillpress.com

Copyright © 2005 by Ruth M. Petrucci

All rights reserved under International and Pan-American Copyright Conventions. With the exception of brief quotations in critical reviews or articles, no part of this work may be reproduced or transmitted in any form or by any means, electronic or mechanical, including photocopying, recording, or any information storage or retrieval system, without permission in writing from the publisher.

Trade Paperback Edition: 1-59408-049-6

1 3 5 7 9 10 8 6 4 2

I
Dedicate This Book
In
Memory of my cat BEAR
October 22, 1998

Pets come in all sizes, breeds, and colors, each with their own unique personality.

> They bring us unconditional love and ask nothing in return.

They know when you are happy or sad, and will stand by you with such understanding and patience.

> Pets can melt your heart like no one else can.

The loyalty of the look in a dog's eyes, and the independence and patience of a cats.

> The playfulness of a puppy or kitten will bring you a lifetime of treasures to remember.

And at the end of the day they will greet you with such enthusiasm as if to say, "I've been waiting for you. Welcome home."

PREFACE

Pets are an important part of the family. You worry about leaving your pet(s) and who will take care of them when you are going away. Getting a reliable pet sitter is the answer. Keeping your pet(s) in the environment they are accustomed will make them happy and comfortable giving you peace of mind.

Pets have always been a part of my life. Growing up I always had one or two cats. They were my companions, best friend and confidant. In later years I had two dogs, a German shepherd mix named Donka and a collie mix named Smokey.

Having a pet is a great way to teach children to care, love, and learn responsibility for another living being besides their families and themselves.

After years of secretarial work I decided I needed a change. I have never regretted my decision and believe it was the best I've ever made. I have never been happier with a job as I am now. It has inspired me to write a book and share my thoughts and experiences with you.

Chapter

1

My First Job

I've had many fascinating experiences in the ten years I've been pet sitting, some happy some sad.

I remember my first job like it was yesterday. I had answered an ad in the newspaper for pet sitting, went on an interview and was hired.

After waiting several weeks, I was finally on my way to meet the clients and their pets. They had three cats that immediately took to me. Their names were Sadie, Daisy and Jezabel. I was to watch them for a long weekend. Besides feeding and playing with the cats, changing their litter box and water dishes, I had other chores to do. I brought in the newspapers, mail and watered the vegetable and flower gardens. Everything worked out beautifully and I was anxiously awaiting more jobs.

Chapter 2

Meeting the Clients

After a client calls, you must set up an appointment to meet with them and their pet(s). One important thing to remember is never keep your client waiting, always be on time.

Having all the information you need is important too. I have an attaché case to keep everything I need in one place. I always keep a pad and pen handy to write down little things about the pet that wouldn't necessarily be in the contract. This meeting is very important, not only do you get the approval of the client but of the pet.

While the contract is filled out, this is an opportune time to play with the pet and get to know him better. I never have a problem entering the house once the client has gone away.

Chapter 3

Preparing for the job

There is a simple procedure that I follow. A contract must be filled out and signed. This gives you all the pertinent information such as:

1. Client's name, address and phone number
2. Name and number of person who can be reached in an emergency.
3. Number that client can be reached at while away.
4. Pets name, breed, age.
5. Where food, treats and medication are kept.
6. Veterinarian used, and if shots are up to date.
7. Length of time client will be gone and the dates.

8. Times for meals, exercise, medication if needed.
9. How many visits per day the pet will need.
10. The following services are provided at no additional cost.

   a) take in the newspaper
   b) answer phone
   c) garbage cans
   d) open and close curtains/blinds
   e) turn on lights
   f) take in the mail
   g) water plants
   h) play TV or radio

The client will let you know just what they want you to take care of besides the pets while they are away.

One client was in an automobile accident and called me from her mothers where she was staying to re-cooperate. She asked if I would care for her Doberman who was at her apartment. I would have to go there alone and meet the dog. I agreed and went to see the dog that morning.

Preparing for the Job

When I arrived I kept calling his name while I unlocked the and opened the door. Once I was inside we became the best of friends after a few dog biscuits and kind words. It is always important to let the dog know you are not afraid of him and that you are his friend.

The dogs name was Teaka, she was a sleek and elegant dog. I always felt safe walking her down the streets. She moved along so proud with long stride-full steps.

Leaving a radio or TV on during the day is not only company for the pet(s) and will make it seem like someone is at home. Having a couple of lights on timers is a good idea, along with leaving different lights on in the house each evening.

What is nice about professional pet sitting is that the pet can stay at his own home and the sitter follows his daily routine. This makes for a very happy pet.

Contentment Is a Cat Napping in the Sun...

Toss a Dog a Stick and He's Your Friend Forever...

Chapter

4

Unexpected Events

Always make sure you have keys that work. Especially if a new key is made for the pet sitter. In all the years I've been sitting, I've only been locked out twice. My first incident happened when I was given only one key and not told about the door knob lock. When leaving I turned the knob and shut the door. I locked the top lock and decided to try both locks when I suddenly realized I only had one key. I could not get back in. Fortunately, I was able to find a window that was unlocked and crawled through while all the pets sat and watched. If only I could have read their minds! The next day I was covered with black and blues.

The second incident happened when my client gave me one key to the front door and then put the dead bolt on by mistake which needed another key to open. Needless to say when I arrived 6:00AM in the morning I couldn't get in. I tried reaching my client on her mobile phone but couldn't reach her. Finally around mid-day I knew I had to feed the dogs and let them out. I found a window off the deck with the screen already torn and pushed back in place. I carefully pulled the screen out enough so I could reach in and open it. I crawled in the window much to the gratefulness of the two dogs. When my client arrived home, I mentioned my predicament to her and she smilingly answered, "Oh we do that all the time".

Unexpected Events

Correct dates are always a must. One client gave me the wrong dates. That's a pet sitter's nightmare. The cat was left alone for the weekend. Fortunately, it was only a short time and the cat had a big bowl of dried food to carry her through. If this was ever a dog, can you imagine the problems there could have been.

One spunky dog I sat for climbed the back yard page fence and just ran around two hours staying just out of my reach. She thought this was quite a game. I finally caught her with the help of our dog warden Jean Murray.

I've had a dog get loose while walking two at a time. It's really difficult to chase a dog when your holding the other one. Now I carry dog biscuits in my coat pocket just in case this happens or if we should meet other dogs on our walk.

One dog had to be lured outside with bits of cheese. He would make it to the back door and poop on the doorstep. It took a while but I finally got him outside before this happened, and he was rewarded with a treat.

Alarms are great. I always feel secure going into a house with an alarm, although dogs can be a great alarm too. I've set off a few, but one in particular comes to mind. I opened the hall door, flicked on the light switch but the bulb had blown out. There I was in total darkness frantically trying to push the correct numbers to no avail. Some pets sit there and give you that "you did it again look," while others run and hide.

I've been dragged through yards, woods, down streets, once got tangled in the dog's leash and fell flat on my face. I've had to carry a Dachshund up and down the stairs to get in and out. Cleaned many a mess from puddles to piles, and it's all part of my job.

Chapter

5

Photographer, Cook and Nurse

I've taken care of diabetic pets that needed daily shots and pets that needed pills for epilepsy. I have always had excellent patients and only had a problem once with a cat who needed a pill. I usually wrap the cat into a large bath towel with just the head out, this way you won't hurt the pet and he won't use you as a human scratching post making his getaway. Some cats will take a pill crushed up and mixed with a tiny bit of tuna or their favorite cat food.

My cat BEAR had to take pills each day for a period of time. He was very lovable each morning while I was in bed, but the minute my feet hit the floor he was gone. He knew what was to follow.

I have several photo albums full of pictures of every pet I've sat for. I usually sit for cats and dogs. I have also sat for rabbits, a variety of birds, an iguana and a pet rat. Each one has their own unique personality and I enjoy all of them.

I have been a special chef at times. I've made hamburgers, microwaved chicken, served shrimp, sardines, scrambled eggs and even Bumble Bee tuna.

Chapter 6

Appointments and Vacations

There have been a couple of times that people have stood me up after setting up an appointment. I've waited outside houses for as long as an hour. After leaving my card with a message they never called me back with an apology or explanation. I find this very thoughtless and inconsiderate especially since I have other jobs and my time is important to me and the pets I am sitting for.

I cover the Hamden, CT area the town I live in and surrounding towns within a certain radius. I have many references if needed. I mainly get jobs now by word of mouth. We do have an excellent backup staff in cases where I'm booked, sick, emergencies or inclement weather.

People have changed their vacation dates so I could sit for their pets. This is quite a compliment and lets me know I'm doing a good job. It is important that clients have peace of mind and their pets are content and happy.

I am very careful to check the house out thoroughly when I leave, especially on the last visit. I cannot control what the pet does once I leave the house. Fortunately most pets are well trained.

Some dogs are easy to take out and walk and do their business. Others will stay out forever and not do a thing. Why do dogs pick the coldest, rainiest or snowy day to just wander around sniffing everything? Of all the cats I've sat for I've only had two that wouldn't come out when I was there to feed them. The only way I knew they were in the house was the flash of a cat zooming by me, the empty food dish and the full litter box.

Appointments and Vacations

Clients have asked if they can call me from their vacations and I always encourage them to do so. If it will put their mind at ease, why not. I've had calls as far away as Sweden, Guadeloupe, California,

Florida, Vermont and as close as a few towns away. While the client is gone I make up a collage and write cute sayings under each photo. I also write a short note about the pet. Everyone is pleased to see what their pet(s) were doing while they were away.

Chapter 7

Losing a Pet

The loss of a pet can be a very traumatic experience. I have lost several wonderful pets and appreciated when friends acknowledged my loss. When a pet dies it is very sad for me too, since I've become so close to them. I was sitting for clients who had a cat that was quite old and didn't have much time left. They were called away on an emergency and asked if I would sit for their pets. I was told the condition of that particular cat. The first two days were fine, I warmed milk with honey and hand fed her some moist food. The third day my worse fear happened. I arrived and found she had died. I put a blanket up to her neck like she was asleep and called the clients and told them what had happened.

They arrived home that afternoon and were grateful for what I did. We have remained special friends and I still sit for their "clan."

I always send a sympathy card and also make a donation to a pet shelter in the pet's memory. Sitting the years I have, I must say there have been quite a few pets that have passed away. I will never forget them, they will live in my heart forever. I've also lost several clients that I was very close to.

Losing clients and their pets because of relocating can be just as sad and a big adjustment for me. I become so attached to the pets that when they leave it's like a part of my family has gone. I have two wirehaired terriers, CP and Daisy. I've been sitting for them six years every Tuesday and Thursday. They moved to the Carolina's and I will never see them again. I do have wonderful memories and lots of pictures of them. Every pet is special in their own way. I'm sure they will miss me too.

Losing a Pet

In Memory Of:

DOGS	CATS
Tasha	Lily
Alexis	Kitty Boy
Libby	Katy
Andy	Spooky

Grigrich	Miss Victoria
Chaps	Chessie
Shadow	Goldie
Lady	Oliver
Rumpy	Oreo
Challanger	Chicklet
Lucky	Misu'
Rainy	Rusty
Joey	Junior
Misha	Gloria
Laurie	BEAR
Sabrina	Bee
Jackson	Tigger
Benson	Lewis
Ebony	Clyde
Sparkle	Cali
Andre	

Chapter 8

Visits

The time spent and the amount of visits varies with each job depending on the number and kinds of pets. Then there are chores that I am asked to do besides taking care of the pet(s). I spend from a half hour to over an hour each visit. Feeding and playtime is very important and I always make sure I spend sufficient time with each pet.

Once you get the routine down everything falls into place. Fenced in yards or invisible fences are great, you can let the pet out to play while you do some chores then go out and play with him. Cats usually stay in during the time the clients are away so you don't have to worry about them spending the night outside. A couple of clients said it was okay if the cat didn't come in, but it bothered me knowing that there are many types of animals roaming around at night. I always made an extra attempt to get the pet in the house.

Cats do not need as much attention as a dog. You can always tell when a cat does not want you to visit and play with them anymore. They just walk away as if you aren't even there. A dog will follow you to the door as if to say "Where are you going?"

Visits

I have a good relationship with all my clients. I had a lovely woman named Ruth Clouse, who fell and broke her hip and was in the hospital for a period of time then sent to a local convalescent home. I made a daily trip to her house to feed her two cats, Miss Victoria and Miss MacNamara during this time.

I spoke to Ruth on the phone and kept her up to date as to how her cats were doing. On Christmas Day she was wasn't going to be home with her cats and told me she was so disappointed and missed them so much. I checked with the supervisor and explained how Ruth wasn't able to be home for Christmas with her cats, so could I please bring Miss Mac in for a visit, she agreed.

That afternoon I walked in with Miss Mac in her carrying case. Ruth started to cry she was so happy and surprised. We took the cat out of the case and she stayed on the bed until it was time to go. Believe it or not even the cat was happy and purring.

It made me feel so good to know that I brought happiness to my friend. She never forgot that visit and I do believe it made her recover much sooner.

Chapter 9

Types of Pets I Sit For

There are many breeds of dogs – Beagles, a feisty one named Kasey, Black Labs, Chocolate Labs, especially Rainy, Bishons, Benson who loved to ride in the car and Misha, Bulldogs and Pugs, Rooney a Boston Terrier, Collies, Cocker Spaniels, Penny and Murphy, Daschunds, Dobermans, German Shepherds, two very beautiful and friendly ones named Sir and Cara. There are poodles, a standard and miniature, Rotweilers, Schnauzers, Huskies, a Samoyed named Apollo, Shelties, a Weimaramer, Golden Retrievers, Topher, Challenger and Ching. A gorgeous Bernese Mountain dog named Bermie. I watch two Portugese Water dogs Beanie and Soshi, a Tibetan Terrier named KC who loves to go for walks. Wired Haired Terriers Daisy and CP. A mixed

Pit Bull breed named Shandy and my longest sweetest client a Cairn Terrier Laurie.

I have never had a problem with any breed of dogs being vicious, if they are trained property from pups they will grow up to be loving gentle creatures.

The variety of cats – I have many tiger cats, Scamp, Toby, Buggsey, Bee, Clyde who loved to chew my hair. Siamese cats named Gus, Tugger and Baby, many lovely Angoras, a Himalian, Ragdolls, beautiful Short Hairs, Thistle, Jack, Arnie, Suke, Toby, Oliver and Tigger. Charles and Albert are real brothers and a delight to watch. Then there are the Calico's Picadilly and Boo.

All these pets are very special to me and have their own special personality.

Pets are my therapy. They keep me happy and are my best friends. My cat BEAR had a unique personality. He brought me unconditional love and asked nothing in return. He knew when I was happy and when I was sad. I loved his patience and strong independence. BEAR brightened up my day and was always happy to see me. He was my best friend and confidant and listener. I've come a long way from my first job. I now have many steady clients. I don't have many free days but I truly enjoy the rewards it brings me. I could never imagine myself being one day without having or caring for a pet.

Types of Pets I Sit For

I've had other types of interesting pets that I sit for, such as an Iguana. He was confined to a cage but I found it very difficult to get to his dishes without being whipped with his strong tail. I finally used cooking tongs to reach in and get his dishes out. Thankfully, he never had to come out of his cage while I took care of him.

I sat for a beautiful parrot named Sam. He was very pleasant and did talk only when he felt like it. Mr. Wiggley was a cockatoo that made a lot of noise. Merlin the lovebird had a mind of his own. I would let him out of his cage while cleaning it and he always tried to bite me. He would actually chase me in the room flapping his wings and his beak wide open. He never did bite, but always tried his best to get me.

Kengi is a cute ferret, that is very playful and friendly. He likes to run around the room when I let him out of his cage and get into all kinds of trouble. He never gives me a problem when he has to go back in his cage because I always give him a treat.

I've sat for two rabbits. One was named Buckwheat, a beautiful brown and white large rabbit. He enjoys his apple a carrot and his dried food. The other rabbit's name is Dolly, a Dutch rabbit with big floppy ears. They are such gentle, sweet pets, she too loved her carrots and apples.

The pet rat was in a large glass aquarium. He just sat there very content and happy eating his food. I didn't have to play with him, just feed him. The owners have moved so I don't get to take care of him anymore.

Cali

I have an outdoor cat named Cali who prefers the freedom of outdoors to the comfort of indoors. She is a beautiful Calico that we found in my neighborhood about fifteen years ago. She was pregnant and had a litter of four lovely kittens. No one could get near Cali so we trapped her along with the kittens. Cali was spayed and returned to my neighborhood, the kittens were fortunate to be placed in good homes. Cali found her way into my yard and my heart, BEAR'S too. They were the best of friends, she was the only cat he allowed in his yard. You will find her sunning herself during the day very content and happy. She comes to the back doorstep each morning, afternoon and evening for her meals. As soon as she finishes she goes on her way enjoying her freedom.

Cali

Bear

On the 22nd of October 1998 my beloved BEAR passed away. There will always be a special place in my heart for him. My newest family are two wonderful cats I adopted from the Connecticut Humane Society.

Actually, BJ picked me out! He was only 14 weeks old and a feisty little guy. As I walked by his cage he started meowing and reached out to touch my leg. I couldn't resist him, so I knelt down and pet him and that was the beginning of a true love affair.

BJ is a Tabby with a charming personality and very inquisitive. Romper is a gorgeous domestic short hair. He was only 12 weeks old. He is very quiet and shy, but both are very lovable in their own way and get along just fine together. Romper loves to curl up on your lap and fall asleep. They both love to touch your face with their paw, in return you kiss their paw and tell them you love them too.

They have their playtime early each morning. It sounds like a herd of horses galloping through the house. My throw rugs are found all curled up in the corners of the room along with their toys.

Their favorite pastime is playing with a leaf bag. It's much bigger than a grocery bag and they can crawl in and play hide and seek. They spend hours every day jumping in and out of this bag. They sleep on it and it in, drag it through the rooms, you never know where you will find it and who will be in it.

BJ loves to watch my Beta Fish named Dawson. He loves to drink the water out of the fish bowl and also takes the artificial plant out of the water with his teeth and tosses it across the room.

They are both great company for me and I am very grateful to have them.

Romper and BJ

Potential Danger To Pets

Bleach

Fertilizers

Aspirin

Ticks & Fleas

Anti-Freeze

Chocolate can be toxic

Letting your dog run free

Cooked chicken, pork, or steak bones

Leaving your pet in a closed car

Small rubber objects to play with

Leaving pet's canned or moist food in dish for prolonged periods.

Be careful with electrical wires

Keep dryer and washing machine doors closed

Poisonous Plants

> Christmas Cherry
> Foxglove
> Horse Chestnut
> Larkspur
> Lily-of-the-valley
> Mistletoe
> Caster Bean
> Lobelia
> Philodendron

Simple Tips on Caring for your Pet

Proper carrying case

Catnip Treats

Rawhide bones

Flea collars

Heartworm pills

Regular checkups with your veterinarian

Give your dog daily exercise and walk

Provide plenty of fresh water

Clean litter box

Brush your pet daily

Nametags are important if they should get lost

Register your dog

Feed your pet where it's quiet so they can enjoy their meal

His/her own bed, pillow, bed basket

Scratching post

Having pet spayed or neutered

Animal Lovers
> Benefits to Pet Sitting

The ideal job...

> Hours are great...
>
>> Plenty of fresh air...
>>
>>> With excellent company...
>>>
>>>> Daily exercise...
>>>>
>>>>> Part time or full time...
>>>>>
>>>>>> Life long relationships...

A pet brings comfort and love to every human if you allow them to...

My Veterinarian is _____
Address   _____
Telephone   _____
Notes   _____

My Pet Sitter is _____
Address   _____
Telephone   _____
Notes   _____

My Breeder is   _____
Address   _____
Telephone   _____
Notes   _____

My Kennel is   _____
Address   _____
Telephone   _____
Notes   _____

My Groomer is   _____
Address   _____
Telephone   _____
Notes   _____

Having a pet keeps you forever young...

A pet brings you unconditional love...

Picture

Name of Pet_____

Date of Birth_____

Breed_____ Sex_____

Markings_____
_____

Favorite Foods_____
_____

Favorite Toys and Pastimes_____
_____
_____

Cats are gentle fur people...

My dog is my best friend...

Picture

Name of Pet_____

Date of Birth_____

Breed_____ Sex_____

Markings_____
_____

Favorite Foods_____
_____

Favorite Toys and Pastimes_____
_____
_____

My Pet is my best confidant and listener...

Contentment is a cat napping in the sun

Highlights and Special Events in My Life

_____
_____
_____
_____
_____
_____
_____
_____
_____
_____
_____
_____
_____
_____
_____
_____
_____
_____

Animals are the spice of life...

Printed in the United States
R1851300005B/R18513PG39685LVSX00007B/